Whispers ON THE Journey

A Practical Guide using the ABCs in Prayer and Praise

BARB SUITER

SE7EN
INTERACTIVE

First Edition

Published by Seven Interactive
1702 Villa Circle
Lebanon, Tennessee 37090

For information regarding permissions or copies purchased for educational or promotional purposes, please email:

Admin@SevenInteractive.com or contact
Seven Interactive, 1702 Villa Circle, Lebanon, Tennessee 37090

Illustrated by Sarah Dean. (See page 111)

For general information about Seven Interactive, please visit SevenInteractive.com.

ISBN: 9798627590141

Unless otherwise noted, Scripture quotations
are taken from the Holy Bible, New International Version.

Dedication

To you, the reader, as you journey this life
in an awareness of His whispers.

To you who long for more,
more of the Father's presence, more of His voice,
I dedicate this book, as you journey this life... listening.

And, to the eternal Whisperer on this journey.

Always listening

Barb Austin

In Gratitude...

My spiritual journey would not be possible without one particular book in my early library. I opened *Disciplines for the Inner Life*, by Bob Benson, Sr. and Michael W. Benson in 1991. I was forever changed. The compilation of readings from the Psalms, of prayers and writings from Christians of centuries past and current, brought an immeasurable dimension into my life which continues.

Further, I say a whispered thank you to 'my baker's dozen prayer girls'. I wish I could whisper sweet words about each one to you; you would love them as I do. Debbie Mills first encouraged me to introduce my ABC way of praise on my blog site. Camille Nelson has been a close friend since high school. Ingrid Graf, Mary Prokop, Nadine Parsi, Vinette Huber in Austria, are four of many reasons I will forever call Vienna 'home'. Inspiration to face challenges on this journey come from prayer friends Jan Murty, Glenda Ferguson, Caprice Cummings, Joyce Messiha, Mandy Workman, and Etta Wicker. How does one travel difficult journeys without praying friends?

Special appreciation is given to Joyce Holleman, one of my baker's dozen, but also for her invaluable attention to the graphic design of this book.

Immeasurable gratitude is given to Amy Bass of Creative Graphics in Lebanon, Tennessee, for her beautiful design of the book.

This small book of a long journey is possible because Rick Edwards, Publisher of Seven Interactive, visualized the possibility of a unique type of devotional book and prayer guide, and encouraged me to finish this project of my journey's walk.

Last, but always first, to my husband, Tom, who whispers encouraging words and who begins breakfast so I can linger longer... listening.

CONTENTS

Whispers of Gratitude and Praise

God Whispers His Love

Whispers in the Heartbreak

Whispers to Personal Desires

Whispers in the Study of God's Word

*W*hat I tell you in the darkness, speak in the light; and what you hear whispered in your ear, proclaim upon the housetops.

Matthew 10:27 NASB

About this book...

I get excited over the ABCs. I mean, really — who gives happy thought to this very basic idea of putting words together with letters. Remember the ABC song? Toddlers dance and swing to the catchy tune long before they recognize the alphabet. However, with teaching and consistent practice, a lifelong language base is assured.

Not only did I learn to read and write with these twenty six letters, I would see a letter or a group of three letters and immediately words came to mind. Composing a phrase with letters on a road sign was my hidden retreat when riding in a car crowded with siblings.

I don't remember the first time I used the ABCs as a focus in prayer and worship. Knowing me, it could have been a day when I had hung sheets out on a windy, spring morning, blowing with promise and joy... and youth. Words of thanksgiving and praise tumbled around me, and suddenly, I began putting them in alphabetical order. "My Father, I praise you because you are... my **A**nchor, my **B**eloved, my **C**omforter... my **J**oy, my **R**eason, my **V**ictory..."

This habit spilled into other areas of life. As a busy pastor's wife and a young mother of two, three, and then four, I soon discovered that I could focus in praise and thanksgiving all day using the ABCs from the list I began in the early morning. At first it was a challenge to conquer every letter with an appropriate word. In those early years, I did not take the time for serious meditation on the words after they found their place beside the exact letter I needed.

I uncovered one of Dr. Billy Graham's secrets. He read five Psalms everyday and one chapter in Proverbs; this assured he would read through the Psalms and the book of Proverbs each month. I can do that, I thought. So began my journey of reading the Psalms devotionally every day. I realize now this simple practice implanted hundreds of words in my mind and heart... of God's character, of His attributes, as well as affirmations of who I am in Him.

For years, this practical exercise has anchored me in worship and praise, bringing structure to my prayers when I was distraught or burdened. Using the ABCs as a guide, I found it easier to concentrate on a particular topic or passage when studying. Years later, I changed my pattern of reading through the Psalms and read every thirtieth Psalm, corresponding with the day of the month. On the fifth of the month, I would read Psalm 5, 35, 65, 95, and 125. Some days, it was uncanny how all five would speak to a particular area in which I needed wisdom or comfort. Other times, I skipped the lamentable Psalms. It would be many difficult life issues later that would cause me to understand those Psalms in a personal way.

Scripture passages in various other studies brimmed with life as I detailed their truth using the ABCs as a study guide. This discipline of spending the first daylight hours listening, pondering what the Lord whispered about Him and about me, ensured my survival years later when heartbreak threatened my faith. At times I could not take the time to read five Psalms. A quick look at Scripture did not birth an ABC list every morning.

In the beginning, making an ABC list was a game... how quickly could I finish a list? I soon discovered the art of listening, hearing whispers from God's heart. I gave thought to the words as they came, and I responded with joy and praise. To sit or walk, focusing on a particular thought, energized my daily life. To hear the heart of God so intimately is a beautiful gift.

A verse or idea would settle me, focus me, as I listened. I identified myself in all the experiences of David, and other writers of the Psalms as they wrote of fear, praise, and doubt. The miracles of Jesus can be studied with this method. I placed myself in Mary and Martha's home. Would I have been in the kitchen fuming or sitting with Jesus... focused?

This continuing practice of applying whispers of ABCs surprises me daily, confirming that the Lord, indeed, is involved in the details of life. Whether I am walking, ironing, or sitting quietly, an initial thought from Scripture, a question, or a phrase from my study comes to mind. Just this morning, reading in Psalm 15... "Who may live on your holy hill?" And the list begins...

These are more than lists. Twenty or twenty-six words are used, yes, but they are more than words. Later in my experience, phrases would come in an alphabetical order. It is the examining of the heart that stills me, forces me to look inwardly, or simply to express praise in a more concentrated manner. Deep thought and concentration using this practice sheds light on a passage I have never before known.

The following lists are but a sampling of my personal journal entries, representing thirty years of my life in praise and doubt. Many of the original pages are yellowed now with sunshine while others are splattered with tears. Heartbreak and doubt are not hidden. I invite you to join me on this simple journey of focus. You will be blessed as you listen to the heart of your Father whispering strong, affirming words over you in your joy or your heartbreak. He, also, will be blessed as you share words of honor and glory to Him.

As a toddler, the practice of learning the ABCs gave me a foundation of speaking and writing. Listening and believing ABC words from Scripture have brought security and focus to my searching heart.

If you have picked up this book, wondering if it will work for you, be assured I am praying it will. Whispers from the Lord's heart, and those from my heart to His, echo on each page to encourage you on your journey. I smile in the hope that you will discover the same joy I have found in listening to and speaking in whispers... with the ABCs as a guide.

Barb Suiter

Lawrenceburg, Tennessee

Helps for Getting Started

First, I listen for a beginning phrase. For example, after reading Psalm 23, I ponder the Lord as my shepherd... *"As my Shepherd, O Lord, you provide me with..."* then from A to Z, whispered words invade my thoughts... **As**-surance, **B**orders, **P**rotection from the enemy, **Q**uiet places, a **S**anctuary.

The initial idea always varies and that determines if I use a verb, a noun, or adjective. *"Create in me a/an _____ heart, O Lord."* In this list, I use an adjective: an **A**ccepting heart, a **B**elieving heart, a **F**aithful heart, a **G**entle heart, a **Y**ielded heart.

Do not fret over finding a word for every letter. The point is to let a word come as you focus on a thought or Scripture. You will see from my lists that Q, X, Y, and Z are especially challenging! You may only have four or five words on your list when you first begin.

You may hear several words for one letter. Sometimes you may use one word for multiple lists. How often I used **Q**uiet for Q! The ABCs keep you on target; an M word could come before you discover a J, but you know you will get back to J, if you want to complete that list. Or maybe not! It is your personal focus that is important.

This is an exercise in listening to an emphasis from Scripture as you venture through your day. There are times when I cannot get past the A in **A**bba... I am too burdened to hear another whisper.

The possibilities are limitless. Scripture vocabulary will increase as you come across words to use in praise, adoration or confession. Words will explode within you as you internalize His voice and express those whispers in praise and thanksgiving. This fundamental, simple guide can encourage a deep awareness of who you are in Christ.

You may want to begin a journal of your words and thoughts with an ABC list. Or you may only want to explore this when walking or dusting, without writing one word. Not only is this a simple, safe exercise, it is a beautiful spontaneous blessing that can work in any language.

I could easily intercede for the peoples of the world the decade we lived and served in Vienna, Austria and Copenhagen, Denmark. Using the ABCs as my prayer guide, my international friends provided me with many names for most letters; there were many Mary's, a Marlene, a Minda, a Maureen, and a Madeleine for the M. I had only one name for the letters I, O, and Y. Ingrid, Osaze and Yemi will never know how often they were remembered!

Walking leisurely or weeding my flower beds provides time for me to pray as I use this method for our extended family. Deliberately and purposely, I begin with our Ahnna, Anita (Tom's sister), Anna and end with my brother William. Every letter but Q, U, V and X, Y and Z is covered. Isaac filled the I spot two years ago. Maybe the next grandchild will be named Victoria or Zoe!

Preparing dinner together with your children is a wonderful time to use the ABCs in an exercise of thankfulness. You can go from Apples or Artichokes to Zucchini quickly. This is a great mental exercise, and an opportunity for teaching children and grandchildren a lesson in praise.

During a recent Christmas break, our family was discussing the possibilities of exploring the ABCs in other areas. Two granddaughters in college laughed, and began noting characteristics they desired in a future husband... from A to Z. Words like Integrity, Kindness, and Valor surfaced. It was fun, yes, but hearing them exclaim over a word, choosing carefully as they shared their desires, made me smile.

If I awaken in the night and can't fall back to sleep, I begin with the ABCs in thanksgiving for the moments of the day or in intercession for family. The next morning I realize I didn't get past the letter C!

Initially you may simply give thought and study to the words whispered on the following pages. Perhaps you will choose a list with multiple scriptures noted beside a word and use it for a devotional study. Whatever method you choose as your beginning, I pray it will bring you **A**bundant joy, **B**lessed peace, and **C**omfort...

When we walk in the Lord's presence,
everything we see, hear, touch
or taste reminds us of Him.
This is what is meant by a prayerful life.

The Living Reminder, Henri J. Nouwen

SECTION ONE

Whispers of Gratitude and Praise

What makes you smile... or want to dance? For me, it's an orange. Every
year my siblings and I found an orange in the toe of our Christmas socks...
the only orange in 365 days. I lived in anticipation of that orange the
whole year! I remember giggling when I peeled the skin and divided the
orange in segments, the juice splattering my freckled face.

Thankfulness colors poverty, a lesson I learned as a child. The gift of an
orange taught me to be thankful. To this day, I enjoy the fragrance and
taste of an orange, and I smile. I didn't know our family was as poor as we
truly were. What I do know is that I was thankful for the small things, the
blue sky days, the flowers, enough food for our large family. I am not sure
you can teach someone to overflow with gratitude, to whisper thank you
for the small gifts of life. Perhaps it was because I had few material things,
I simply was grateful for the everyday miracles.

Out of gratefulness, I began to praise. The Psalmist counsels us to "give
thanks to Him and praise His name" after inviting us to "enter His gates
with thanksgiving and His courts with praise" Psalm 100:4. Thanking
Him precedes praise.

My ABC lists in thanksgiving often begin with a serendipitous moment.
On one page I have written, "the wonder of it all" as I watched the sun
creep to a brilliant explosion that particular early morning. I quickly
found words to express thankfulness for the morning's gifts; then I
continued in praise.

In this section, lists of praise are sandwiched between those of thanksgiving. Praise is a natural result of being grateful; I'm convinced you can't have one without the other. I encourage you to be attentive to the moments that delight you, to be sensitive to the world around you and stand in the wonder that our Creator God is worthy of praise.

Then beginning with an A... **Awesome, Almighty** *(whisper your words to Him)*... continuing to Z.

Whatever joys your heart, brightens your day, lightens your burdens... when evidence of God's majestic power explodes within you, I encourage you on page 42 to let words of thankfulness and praise dance around you in alphabetical order.

It is difficult for me, and I am certain, for you, to express words of thankfulness and praise during the storms of life. Section Three (page 66) in this book may help guide you through those times.

"I will praise God's name in song
and glorify Him with thanksgiving."
Psalm 69:30

I began to learn the ways of God and who He wanted to be in my life by affirming Him with these meditative lists. Through a growing awareness of who He was, I became confident and secure in His love. The topic of praise occurs over and over in my journals and in multiple lists. Even when I am discouraged, I can glorify Him with the ABCs.

My Father and Lord, You are...

Always

    Almighty

my Burden Bearer

Creator   Isaiah 40:28

Divine

    my Deliverer   Psalm 6:4

Exalted

    my Everything

Faithful

    my Friend

Good

Holy

the I Am of life!   Exodus 3:14

    Involved in my life

Jealous

King

Lord of all

    Light   Love   Life

Majestic

Near   Psalm 73:28

the Only One

Peace

    my Protector

Quiet in Your love

Righteous

    my Rock   my Restorer

Salvation

    my Strength   Sweetness

Truth

Unchangeable

Victorious

Wisdom

    Worthy   Welcoming

X

Y

Z

"Praise the Lord, O my soul;
all my inmost being, praise His holy name."
Psalm 103:1

The Desire of My Heart

*M*y Pollyanna spirit colors most mornings with hope. I begin the day with freedom and thankfulness that *"God's in His heaven — All's right with the world."** I celebrate the Lord's presence in life... in these moments. I open hands and heart to receive instruction for the day's journey.

Father, the desire of my heart is to...

Adore You   Psalm 119:171

Believe in You

Commune with You

Draw near to You

Exalt You

Find You in the moments   Psalm 119:32

Give You my burdens

    Glorify You in all I do

Hide You in my heart   Psalm 119:11

Imitate Your ways

Joy in Your presence

Kneel before You

Laugh in celebration of Your love

Meditate in Your Word   Psalm 119:16, 97

Never complain

Open my eyes to see You in the details   Psalm 119:18

Practice Your presence

Quickly obey

Renew my mind

Surrender to Your will

Trust You in the difficulties

Understand others

Value others

Worship You in praise

X

Yield my will to You

Z

Notice how these verses from Psalm 119 speak of the biblical author's desire to praise and obey the Lord!

"Let the morning bring me word of Your unfailing love,
for I have put my trust in You. Show me the way
I should go, for to You I lift up my soul."
Psalm 143:8

*Robert Browning, *Pippa Passes*

I enjoy early mornings that awaken me with peace and security. We had been in Europe for almost a year and a half. I sometimes wondered if our adult children were managing life with us so far away. Conversations on Skype the night before reassured us all was well. Confident the Lord is guarding their lives as He is ours, I skip with joy down my secret path this lovely July morning of 2003 in Vienna.

In an attitude of wonder there is a longing within me to...

Acknowledge You as Creator

Bring You pleasure

Celebrate You in these moments

Develop a constant awareness of You

Expect You in the moments

Fill my mind with a sense of Your purpose

Give you my dreams

Honor You with my words

Involve You in all decisions

Joy in Your presence

Keep Your face before me

Listen to Your heart

Miss nothing in this day

Notice Your creative works

Obey You

Please You

Quiet my spirit before You

Reflect on all things good

Sit at Your feet

Take Your hand and trust that You are always here

Use my time wisely

Verify Your Word in me

Willingly surrender

X-press my devotion

Yield all of me to You

Z

"A heart at peace gives life to the body..."
Proverbs 14:30a

*H*igh temperatures and no air conditioning were reasons to keep windows covered and shutters closed during Vienna's heat wave of 2003. While the dimness did create a sense of coolness, it darkened my spirit after several days. How refreshing to open the door early one July morning for light breezes to blow in. I grabbed my sweat shirt, and made a dash to the garden path. Sensing His love and presence, I began.

My Father, I simply walk in...

an Awareness of Your presence

the Beauty of Your creation

the Comfort of knowing You

the Delight of this day

an Excitement of You in this day

the Freshness of this morning

Gratitude of Your gifts

Honesty with You

Intimate conversation with You

Joy

the Knowledge of who You are

Your Light and Love

the Moments

Your Nearness

an Offering of self

Praise

the Quietness of this place

Remembrance

the Security of Your promises

a Trust of the future

Union with You

V

the Wonder of this day

X

the Yoke with You

Z

"I run in the path of Your commands,
for You have set my heart free."
Psalm 119:32

Who Do You Say That I Am?

*M*ornings awaken quieter and colder some days; I don't walk. I sense a need to listen. It's as if I have an appointment, and I can't be late. The only note I have written at the bottom of this journal page on a December day reveals I was focusing on a thought... "the red of a cardinal on the frozen, crystallized ground." What was I dreaming? Maybe it was thankfulness to see bright color on the cold carpet. Whatever it was, I heard a whisper, "Barb, who do you say I am in your life?" And the ABCs took off.

Jesus, You are...

Ancient awe

the Breath of this season

Christmas

the Divine Deliverer

Eternal

Freedom

Grace

Hope

the Incarnation of the Father

Joy

Knowledge

Life

    Love   Light   Lord   Laughter

Messiah

Now

the Only One

Peace

Quiet love

the Reason to celebrate

Salvation

Truth

   Triumph   Time

Understanding

the Voice

Warmth

   the Word

X

Y

Z

"But what about you?"
He asked. "Who do you say I am?"
Simon Peter answered, "You are the Christ,
the Son of the living God."
Matthew 16:15-16

THIS DAY, I THANK YOU FOR...

*W*ords swirled around me like snowflakes this morning in June. It would definitely be a rare day with snow this hot month. I was so overwhelmed with His goodness and gifts that I danced in gratitude. I quote this line often from James Russell Lowell's poem, *The Vision of Sir Launfal*, "what is so rare as a day in June" when the skies are deep blue, and I overflow with thankfulness.

This day, O Lord, I thank you for...

Abilities

    Anticipation   Answers to prayer

Birds

Choices

    Clouds

Dreams

Energy

Flowers

    Friends   Freedom   Fragrance

Gardens

    Grandchildren

Home

Intimacy in marriage

Jars *(I love jars!)*

Kind people

Laughter

    Love   Lilacs

Mornings

    Mountains   Memories

Nature

Opportunities

    Oranges *(I love oranges!)*

Poetry

Quietness

Rainbows

    Rain   Roses   Rest

Sunrises

    Sunsets   Silence

Tom

    Trees   Touch

Umbrellas

Variety

    Vacations

Wind

    Words

X

Y

Z

"This is the day the Lord has made;
I will rejoice and be glad in it."
Psalm 118:24 *(personalized)*

You Are My...

I walk calmly into a windy April morning. Allowing the pain of yesterday to blow away, I only desire to treasure the Lord for who He is in my life this day. I whisper to the Lord, "Because of Your goodness, I am grateful."

You are my...

Answer

Blessing

Calmness

Delight

Everything

Friend

Gain

  Goal

Hiding place

Ideal

Joy

Keeper

Lamp

Mirror

Name

Own

Peace

Quest

Reason

Silence

Tomorrow

Unchangeableness

Victory

Wisdom

X-pression

Y

Z

There are times in my journals where no Scriptures are referenced on a list. But yet the whispered words come from past studies. Sometimes I look up a Scripture, but more often, I remember and ponder the truth of a word.

"Be joyful always; pray continually;
give thanks in all circumstances,
for this is God's will for you in Christ Jesus."
I Thessalonians 5:16-18

*H*eavy frost sparkled the lawn with cold jewels; I was not about to brave the frigid temperature. Wrapped in my favorite blanket, sipping a hot tea, I focused on the truth that the Lord plans good for me even on cold days. The study of Psalm 18 this morning was full of praise as David sang to the Lord, prompting me to begin.

I will praise you, O Lord, for you have...

Armed me with strength

Broadened my path, so I will not fall

Confided in me   Psalm 25:14

Determined good for me

Enabled me to stand

Filled my heart with gladness

Given me Your shield of victory

Held me in times of trouble

Invaded my life with Your goodness!

Justified me

Kept me

Lifted me up

Made me see wonderful works

Never let me go

Offered me life

Purposed that I be holy

Q

Released me from fear and guilt

Set me free

Turned my darkness into light

Unleashed lavish love on me

Voluntarily given Your life for me

Whispered Your presence

    Watched over me

X

Y

Z

These thoughts and phrases are easily discovered as you treasure this Psalm.

"You give me Your shield of victory,
and Your right hand sustains me;
You stoop down to make me great."
Psalm 18:35

A steady drizzle grayed the May dawn. I snuggled under the security of my umbrella, welcoming God's presence as the drops danced in rhythm over me. Tom and I walked under an umbrella on our first date. It is a lovely memory, and I still enjoy times when I can walk slowly, comforted by this cover. I reflected on ways the Lord is a protector during the rainy days in life. Words splattered over me.

Father, You are my...

Anchor

Banner

Covering

Dwelling place

Eternal security

Fortress   Psalm 91:2

Guard

Hiding place

Island... in the midst of a vast ocean

Jewel of hope

Key to life

Lamp to light the way

Mountain top

North Star

Oasis

Protector   Psalm 25:20

Quiet place

Rock   Psalm 71:3

Shelter

Tent

Umbrella

Vision

Wings of protection   Psalm 63:7-8

X

Y

Z

"He will cover you with His feathers,
and under His wings you will find refuge... "
Psalm 91:4a

I Come to You

*N*othing has changed; the same stress of yesterday is here today. For some reason, I am more aware of the Lord's presence. Burdens weigh lighter. Morning dawns with brilliant promises, and I waltz into a new day.

I eagerly come to You, my Lord...

in Awe

in Boldness

with Confidence

with the Desires of my heart

in Expectation

First and finally!

in Gratitude

Humbly

Intimately

Joyfully

Keenly aware of who You desire to be in my life

Listening for Your whispers

Meditating on Your promises

Needing a fresh word

Opened

Panting for Your presence

Quite contented

Rejoicing in this day

Singing of Your love

Trusting You for answers

Unwavering in hope

V

Welcoming You

X

Yielded to Your will

Z

"Surely God is my help;
the Lord is the One who sustains me."
Psalm 54:4

I Worship You, Creator God

A flock of Canadian geese just flew over... right above my window, and I rush to open the door. The blaring honks to each other awaken a wonder in my heart I can't explain. The loud commands ensure order on their journey as they shift leaders in their V-formation. There go 'my geese', I always say. Watching these graceful creations this morning, I stand in awe. The Creator has directed even the birds to migrate north and south in the appropriate seasons...

I worship You, Creator God.
Today I choose to...

Adore You with my whole heart

Bring You glory

Celebrate life in You

Delight You with my words and thoughts   Psalm 37:4

Exemplify You in all my actions

Follow You even when I don't 'see'

Give thanks in everything

Hold Your hand through this day   Psalm 73:23

Include You in life

Joyfully serve You

Know You hear me   Psalm 18:6

Live today for Your pleasure

Make You smile

Never grieve Your heart

Obey Your words

Praise You continually   Psalm 71:8

Quiet my spirit in Yours

Release my worries

Surrender all of me to all of You!

Trust You with everything   Psalm 37:3

Unite my will wholly with Yours

V

Walk in Your ways

X

Y

Z

"O Lord, our Lord,
how majestic is Your name in all the earth!"
Psalm 8:1

How Will You Focus Your Praise and Gratitude?

This is your page, expressing praise to your Lord using the alphabet. Perhaps the day overflows with all things good. Praise erupts as you sense His presence and peace in these moments. You whisper to Him words or phrases of who He is. You might say, "Lord, You are..." or you could say, "Lord, You are my..." or even, "Lord, You have... A–Z." Remember, you are not compelled to complete a list, but to use the ABC order to focus on praise.

_____ ◄ ◄

A _____

B _____

C _____

D _____

E _____

F _____

G _____

H _____

I _____

J _____

K _____

L _____

M _____

N _____

O _____

P _____

Q _____

R _____

S _____

T _____

U _____

V _____

W _____

X _____

Y _____

Z _____

"It is good to praise the Lord
and make music to Your name, O Most High,
to proclaim Your love in the morning,
and Your faithfulness at night."
Psalm 92:1

Identify a verse that is personal to you this day.

_____

_____

_____

There must be always remaining in every man's life
some place for the singing of angels, some place for that which in itself
is breathlessly beautiful... life is saved by the singing of angels.

Deep Is the Hunger, Howard Thurman

SECTION TWO

God Whispers His Love

"I have never heard anyone say that many good words over me," a sweet Christian lady smiled with tears. She had read an ABC list of what God had whispered to me, and yes, the whispers had touched her spirit, too. Pat wiped her tears, and said, "I had no idea I was that special to Him." She has been a believer for more than forty years.

Brennan Manning writes in *Ragamuffin Gospel,* "There is one question the Lord will ask, 'Do you believe I loved you... just as you are, just as you were?'" He adds, "I am a recovering alcoholic—on and off the wagon..." Manning, a former Catholic priest, transparent of his life struggles, shared from Wall Street to Nairobi, Kenya, that "the god of so many Christians I meet is a god who is too small for me."

Do you really believe this immortal, eternal, Creator God loves you... for who you are? Even when you fall off the wagon? Each one of us is recovering from something... It took years to understand and really know God could love me. It was difficult to receive His love as I missed proper affection and affirmation as a child. As an adult, I slowly found acceptance and security when I began focusing and believing His whispered words about me. I would ponder a completed ABC list of assurance again and again. I began to understand His love.

Imagine my joy one morning when I read Isaiah 49:16. I knew my mother loved me, but our relationship was often strained. The prophet in this passage had just asked if a mother could forget a child at her breast. Yes, she may forget, but the Lord will not forget me or you. Then the Lord breathed this glorious promise: "Behold, I have indelibly imprinted or tattooed a picture of you on the palm of each of My hands." *(Amplified)*

Pages in my old journals tell my story of falling on and off the wagons of guilt, doubt and insecurity. What about you? Are you confident that the Creator who shouts the thunder also whispers your name? This God whispers to you, "You are the apple of My eye."

The words on the following pages are mine. You will use your words; they will be yours, personal to you. Some may, of course, be the same as those I have used. He loves each one of us and longs to whisper words of truth over us. As you reflect on my words or phrases, let them be a guide, a beginning. You can then create your own list on page 64.

"For God so loved the world that He gave His one and only Son,
that whoever believes in Him shall not perish
but have eternal life."
John 3:16

*A*BC lists of personal affirmation are found scattered in my older journals. Now I realize I required more assurance in my early years that my Creator Father loved me... for me. Childhood abuse had convinced me I was not worth much. There were days I needed to hear again His whispers of acceptance.

Because You love me, my Father, I am...

Accepted

Beloved

Chosen   Ephesians 1:4

Desired

Examined   Psalm 139:23

Forgiven

Guarded   Psalm 25:20; 121:5-6

an Heir   Romans 8:17

Intricately made   Psalms 139:13-14

Justified

Kept   Isaiah 42:6

Loved   John 3:16

Made in Your image

Named   Isaiah 43:1; 45:3

One with You

Planned for   Jeremiah 29:11

Quiet in Your love   Zephaniah 3:17

Restored

   Renewed

Set apart   Jeremiah 1:5

Trusting

Useful

Victorious

Woven together beautifully!

X-onerated!

Yours

Zealous

There is a word for every letter of the alphabet in this list. This makes a great Bible study when you need biblical evidence of what the Lord says about you.

"But because of His great love for *me*,
God, who is rich in mercy,
made *me* alive with Christ even when *I* was dead
in transgressions — it is by grace
I have been saved."
Ephesians 2:4-5 *(personalized)*

I Am Your Shepherd

I was perched on our rock wall, stretching before my walk. I imagined sheep in the field below, but especially today. I had thought long this morning on the promises of the 23rd Psalm. It was as if the Lord quietly spoke, "Listen as I declare my care of you." Can you imagine how intimate it is to hear the 23rd Psalm quoted by the Shepherd? "I am your Shepherd, Barb. You will not want, I will lead you, I will guide you..." Oh, did my cup spill over with gladness that morning. I walked, hearing whispers of the Shepherd's care.

I am your Shepherd. I give you...

Assurance

Borders

Comfort   Psalm 23:4

    Confidence

Direction

Emotional healing   Psalm 23:5

Freedom from fear   Psalm 23:4

Guidance through this maze of life   Psalm 23:3

Help, even before you call

Instruction for today

Journey joys

Knowledge

Leadership

Moment by moment care

Nearness of My presence

an Oasis in the storm

Protection from the enemy

Quiet places   Psalm 23:2

Restoration   Psalm 23:3

Safety through the valleys   Psalm 23:4

Teachings for life

Unfailing love

Victory in the circumstance

Warnings

X

Y

Z

The ABC method makes a great exercise for this Psalm.

"He tends His flock like a shepherd;
He gathers the lambs in His arms
and carries them close to His heart;
He gently leads those that have young."
Isaiah 40:11

BARB, YOU ARE...

*T*om surprised me with roses yesterday; he smiles, hugs me, and whispers, "You do know how much I love you?" Evidence of his love often comes with a gift he made in his shop or in a written note. Tom's expressions of love over these years reinforced God's unfailing love to my insecure heart. I understood and accepted God's love as I experienced Tom's love. I smile at the "roses" my Creator Father gives me daily as I accept the truth of His whispers.

Barb, you are...

the Apple of My eye	Deuteronomy 32:10
Blameless	Ephesians 1:4
Chosen	John 15:16
My Delight	Psalm 18:19
Empowered	
Forgiven	Acts 10:43
Given grace	Ephesians 4:7
Honored in My sight	Isaiah 43:4
Imprinted on the palm of My hand	Isaiah 49:16
my Joy	Zephaniah 3:17
a King's daughter	
a Letter from Christ	2 Corinthians 3:2-3
Mine!	Isaiah 43:1b
a New creation	2 Corinthians 5:17
One with Me	John 17:21
Precious to Me	Isaiah 43:4
Q	

Rich with an inheritance	Ephesians 1:18
Reconciled	2 Corinthians 5:18
Redeemed	Psalm 71:23
Sealed	2 Corinthians 1:22
a Treasure	
Unique	Psalm 139:14
Victorious	
Washed clean	
X	
Y	
Z	

There are many positive words you could add to this list. This makes a delightful study.

"Many, O Lord my God, are the wonders You have done.
The things You planned for us no one can recount to You;
were I to speak and tell of them,
they would be too many to declare."
Psalm 40:5

*W*orries have a way of changing my focus, even as I awaken. I admit doubt and fear can take swift possession of intended worship. It is in these early moments I must choose my direction for the day. I determine to listen to His familiar voice and hear Him speak.

Focus on the important; you only need to...

Ask Me

Believe Me

Call to Me

Desire Me

Expect Me

Follow Me

Give Me your worries

Hold My hand

Imitate Me

Join Me in serving

Keep My word in your heart

Leave your burdens with Me

Mend any broken relationship

Notice Me in your surroundings

Obey My commands

Please Me

Quiet your mind

Rejoice in today

Seek My face

Tell others

Use your hands to bless others

V

Walk with Me through this day

X-pand your mind

Yearn for Me

Z

"In the morning, O Lord, You hear my voice;
in the morning, I lay my requests before You
and wait in expectation."
Psalm 5:3

*F*orgive me, Lord, for having a pity party this week and believing the devil's insinuations I am not worthy of Your grace and riches. A failure has devastated me, driving me into morbid despair of who I am. Now, after sitting here at Your feet, I listen as You whisper Your heart for me.

I have surely blessed you with countless gifts. You have...

an Amazement for life

a love for Beauty

Creativity

a Desire for Me

Experiences to share

Family

> Friends   Faith

undeserved Grace

Hands for work

Introspection

Joy

Knowledge

Love for others

> Laughter   Life

Memories

A love for Nature

an Observant eye

Peace

a Quest for more of Me

Rest

Serendipity

Tom *(this one makes me dance)*

a Useful purpose

Victory

Work

X-pectation for today

a Yearning for Me

Zest for living

There are no empty spaces for any letter! Why do I doubt His love and acceptance? God is so beautiful in affirming the truth that I am His, and His love is forever the same.

"You have not handed me over
to the enemy but have set my feet
in a spacious place."
Psalm 31:8

As Your Anchor, I Will...

C hange was coming. We had served the International Baptist Church in Vienna for six years as pastor and wife. I treasured every day, every person. When the decision was made by our mission board that the church become self-supporting, I was devastated and unprepared for the next step. We were to minister elsewhere in the city, but what would we do? Worry prevented me from trusting. This beautiful morning in September of 2006, I opened my heart to hear the Lord's promises.

As your anchor, I will...

Answer, always

Bless you

Calm your spirit

Direct you

Engrave your picture on My hand   Isaiah 49:16

Fellowship with you

Give you the desires of your heart   Psalm 21:2

Hear you   Psalm 18:6

Intercede for you   Romans 8:27

Justify you

Keep you

Lift you up   I Peter 5:6

Make your plans succeed   Psalm 20:4

Never, never let you go   Hebrews 13:5

Open your eyes

Protect you

Quiet you in My love

Restore your joy   Isaiah 55:12

Surround you

Teach you

Use you and Tom

Validate you

Watch over you   Psalm 121:5

X

Y

Z

We continued in Vienna for two years, serving and ministering in conferences and Bible studies while strengthening the ongoing work that had begun years earlier at the United Nations building. The Lord truly directed our journey.

"I am the Lord your God,
who teaches you what is best for you,
who directs you in the way you should go."
Isaiah 48:17b

The Lord Gives Me Hope

*M*y mind was saturated with verses from Isaiah. I had been teaching a series from one of my favorite Old Testament books. Words of affirmation brightened my morning walk after pondering Isaiah 43. Isaiah, the prophet, had given the people of Israel hope after his serious rebuke in previous verses. I wanted my ears opened to hear this same God declare His unfailing love.

I have...

Accepted you

    Appointed you

Blessed you

Called you   Isaiah 43:7

    Created you

Delivered you

Enabled you

    Entrusted you

Formed you   Isaiah 43:1

    Filled you   Freed you   Forgiven you

Guarded you   Isaiah 52:12

    Gifted you

Held you   Isaiah 42:6

Imprinted you on the palm of My hand   Isaiah 49:16

Justified you

Kept you   Isaiah 42:6

Loved you   Isaiah 43:4

Made you   Isaiah 43:7

Nurtured you

Offered you freedom
Planned good for you   Jeremiah 29:11
    Prepared a place for you   John 14:2
Quenched the fire around you   Isaiah 43:2
Redeemed you   Isaiah 43:1
Summoned you by name
    Set you apart   Jeremiah1:5
Trusted you
    Taught you   Isaiah 54:13
Unburdened you
V
Watched you
X
Yoked you with Me
Z

"I will give you the treasures of darkness,
riches stored in secret places,
so that you may know that I am the Lord,
the God of Israel, who summons you by name."
Isaiah 45:3

One morning on the 26th of the month, I read Psalm 26 and then read every thirtieth Psalm, a practice I continue to use at times. ABC thoughts surfaced rapidly as I read Psalm 26, 56, 86, 116, and 146. Parallel statements of the Lord's many attributes of goodness appeared. The phrase 'abounding in love' was an easy A as I let the words of Scripture spill over me.

He whispers, I am...

Abounding in love and faithfulness	Psalm 86:5, 15
Bringing joy	
Comforting you	
Delivering you	Psalm 86:13
Defending you	
Eternal	
Forgiving you	Psalm 86:5
Guarding your life	Psalm 86:2
Helping you	
Instilling My desires within you	
Jealous for you	
Knowing your thoughts	
Lighting your path	
Lifting you up	
Merciful	
Never far away	
Omnipotent	
Protecting you	Psalm 116:6
Q	
Reigning forever	

Setting you free... today   Psalm 116:16

Teaching you My way   Psalm 86:11

Upholding you by My right hand

Victorious

Watching over you   Psalm 146:9

X-treme in My love   Psalm 86:13

Yoked with you

Z

"For You are great and do marvelous deeds;
You alone are God."
Psalm 86:10

The Scriptures persuade that Christ lives and breathes in me. As I considered this fundamental truth, I was overwhelmed with the characteristics and ways of Christ I am to imitate. "In this world we are like Him" (I John 4:17b). These thoughts came after a concentrated parallel study in the books of Colossians and Philippians. The life I am to live in Christ is so clearly magnified in these two letters to the young churches. My walk this day led me to hear His whispers of how I am to look and act.

You are to be like Me in...

Attitude	Philippians 2:5
Boldness	
Confidence	
Compassion	
Desire	
Example	
Experience	
Forgiveness	Colossians 3:13
Gentleness	
Hope	
Image	Colossians 3:12-13
Joy	
Knowledge	Colossians 1:10; 2:8
Love	
Mind	
Name	
Openness	

Patience   Colossians 1:11

    Purity

Quest

Reason

Song

Truth

Understanding

Victory

Walk

    Wisdom

X

Y

Z

"This is how we know we are in Him:
Whoever claims to live in Him
must walk as Jesus did."
I John 2:5b, 6

*F*or years, I have read Scripture personally, as if the words were speaking directly to me. I change the 'you or us' to read 'I and we'. I make the words for the Lord personal, too. You will then understand why my favorite verse in the entire Bible is Ephesians 1:4. The Amplified version and my personalization of that verse declare: "Even as in Your love, my God, You chose me — actually picked me out for Yourself as Your own — in Christ before the foundation of the world; that I should be holy, consecrated and set apart for You..." (*Amplified and personalized*). Let your mind wander and wonder! Listening to your Father's whispers, begin with an A... it could be the Apple of His eye, or it might be Accepted. Let your words come.

Father, because You love me, I hear you whisper, _____, you are...
(your name)

A _____

B _____

C _____

D _____

E _____

F _____

G _____

H _____

I _____

J _____

K _____

L _____

M _____

N _____

O _____

P _____

Q _____

R _____

S _____

T _____

U _____

V _____

W _____

X _____

Y _____

Z _____

"Fear not,
for I have redeemed you;
I have summoned you by name;
you are Mine."
Isaiah 43:1b

Find a beautiful verse of promise, just for you.

_____

_____

_____

What would happen to us
if we would more deeply believe the truth
— God speaks! God speaks to me! This is the heart of prayer,
this is the power behind the prayer revolution of today —
that God is speaking directly to me in Scripture.

Prayer Is a Hunger, Edward J. Farrell

SECTION THREE

Whispers in the Heartbreak

It is easy to praise the Lord in the sunshine. Even on cloudy days, one can praise and be thankful. But consider… what about the days blackened with pain; when there is no answer? Is it possible to praise?

A few years ago, circumstances caused a deep break in our family. I realized my simple, childlike faith was not as strong as I had believed. I had been so 'innocent', so sure God would always make life good. My belief and trust in God were unshakeable. At times, I was even guilty of judging those who found it impossible to trust in such an awesome God. After all, God is good all the time, I uttered sanctimoniously.

*"God whispers to us in our pleasures, speaks to us in our conscience, but shouts to us in our pain; it is His megaphone to rouse a deaf world."** I would add He also *whispers* to us in our pain, if we listen.

My world was shaken. I learned I had no idea what real trust was. I grasped the sad truth that I desired God's goodness more than I desired Him. A long, dark journey began as I struggled to find this good God in my pain.

What does one do with divorces of adult children… How do I cope with the broken relationships and the loss of precious grandchildren in the sweet role as Gram I had enjoyed? Life as Tom and I had known was forever altered. Please God, can't You fix this? I crumbled in Tom's arms like a brittle cookie; he tried to hold the pieces together.

There were times I could only read one verse of scripture, but I would hear the Lord whisper, "Barb, I am here." The King can and will put the pieces together. No, the solution I ached for and prayed for never happened in either situation. Trust is being confident God is still here, present in this pain, and He will be here tomorrow, regardless of what happens.

The pain of loss is still with me, but He is the same. It has been kindergarten all over for me in this lesson of trust. I continue to grow. *"Only when we discover a desire for Him that is stronger than our desire for relief from pain will we pay the price necessary to find Him."***

Worries often choke the joy of the future. I forget for a moment He is and will always be right here, putting my broken life together. I listen again to His whispers, hearing ABC words as He promises me His presence.

The following ABC lists are the Lord's whispers to me, and mine to Him, during periods of doubt and unbelief. Perhaps you can hear His whispers in your pain, using the ABCs as your guide.

"Have mercy on me, O God, have mercy on me,
for in You my soul takes refuge. I will take refuge in the shadow
of Your wings until the disaster has passed."
Psalm 57:1

*C.S. Lewis, *Problem of Pain*, p. 91
** Larry Crabb, *Shattered Dreams*, p. 100

*I*t wasn't God's goodness I doubted; it was not that I had lost faith. Or maybe I had. I questioned that our daughter would 'find the Lord's way' again as she had been going her own way for a couple of years. Her choices had broken our family. Thankfully, her heart and life were restored to us after three years. In her struggle to find God anew, these words groaned from my heart...

Please, Lord, grant _____ *a new...*
          (child's name)

Awareness of who You are

Beginning

Commitment for You

Desire for You

Enthusiasm for life

Freedom in her faith

Gift of grace

Hunger for You

Insight into Your heart for her

Joy in You

Knowledge of You

Love for You

Marriage relationship

Nobleness

Openness with You

Purpose in life

Quest for more

Rest in You

Serenity

    Song to You

Thirst for You

Usefulness

Vision of You

Word from You

X-citement

Yieldedness of self

Zeal for You

This list is complete from A to Z! There are hundreds of words you can pray for your children. I made the verse below a prayer for years, inserting our daughter's name in the place of 'you'. Now I am praying a new list for another child.

"I keep asking that the God of our Lord Jesus Christ,
the glorious Father, may give you the Spirit of wisdom
and revelation, so that you may know Him better.
I pray also that the eyes of your heart
may be enlightened in order that you may know the hope
to which He has called you, the riches
of His glorious inheritance in the saints,
and His incomparably great power
for us who believe."
Ephesians 1:17-19b

TODAY, I WILL...

*R*etirement from our mission board presented us with both uncertainties and excitement. We returned to the states with dreams of another ministry. What was ahead? At times we were confident the Lord had prepared a place for us, but still, there loomed doubt. We were to receive compensation for several months due to accrued time, but soon that would be spent. It wasn't too difficult standing firm during these early months, believing that answers would come. I promised Him my commitment to trust early in April of 2010.

Today, O Lord, I will . . .

Abide with You

Believe Your words

Commit to walk in Your steps

Delight to do Your will

Expect good from You

Fix my eyes on You   Psalm 141:8

Give honor and praise for who You are in my life

Hold You in my heart

    Hear Your voice

Imagine Your plan

Joyfully wait

Keep my focus on You

Lift my eyes to see You   Psalm 121

Make known to others what You have done

Not despair

Obey Your commandments

Pour out my desire to You   Psalm 142

Quiet my heart before You

Rest in You

Sing a new song

    Seek You with my whole heart

Trust in Your unfailing love

Understand (*I will try to understand this wait*)

Visualize Your goodness

Walk in freedom

    Wait on You

X-pect great things

Yield to Your will

Z

"For I know the plans I have for you,
declares the Lord,
plans to prosper you and not to harm you,
plans to give you a hope
and a future."
Jeremiah 29:11

*T*he previous ABC list was my commitment to trust the Lord concerning our future. By midsummer of 2010, our savings were slipping away and income limited. Believing the Lord's promises was difficult; worries robbed my peace. My faith wavered. Even as I sought the Lord's face for His direction, I was fearful. I confess, this was a most challenging time to trust. This list is my attempt in confidence.

I trust You, Lord, that surely You will...

Answer

Bless us with the right place

Calm me

Delight in us

Engrave my face in Your heart   Isaiah 49:16

Fellowship with us

Grant us the desire of our heart

Hold me in Your right hand

Instruct me in the way I should go   Psalm 25:12

J

Keep us safe

Listen   Psalm 10:17

    Light our way

Make all our plans succeed   Psalm 20:4

Never, never let us go   Hebrews 13:5b

Open my eyes to see Your truth

Protect us   Psalm 5:11

Quiet me

Restore unto me the joy of trusting You

Shelter us with Your presence

Test me *(You definitely are in these moments)*

Uphold us   Psalm 41:12

Validate us

Watch over us

X

Y

Z

Jesus replied, "I tell you the truth,
if you have faith and do not doubt,
not only can you do what was done to the fig tree,
but also you can say to this mountain, 'go,
throw yourself into the sea,' and it will be done.
If you believe, you will receive
whatever you ask for in prayer."
Matthew 21:21-22

YOU ARE MY...

*F*ive months had passed since the two previous entries concerning a ministry or employment after retirement. No lightning bolts; no telegrams from the hand of God. Nothing. How do we make it tomorrow? What happens next? We were surviving, but that was all. Desperately, I tried to hold on to my faith. Through tears, this rainy September morning of 2010, I cry.

Today, oh Lord, I want to, I want to believe that You are still my _____ in life.

Anchor

Burden bearer

Creator

Dwelling

Escape

Faithful Friend

Guide   Psalm   142:3

Hiding Place   Psalm 32:7

I am!

Joy

Keeper

Loving God   Psalm 33:21-22

Moment!

Need

Oasis

Promise

Quietness

Rock   Psalm 18:31

Strong Arm

Tower

Umbrella

Victory

Watchman

X

Y

Z

Tom was offered a part time ministry opportunity a few days later, which led to a full-time position.

"I am convinced and sure of this very thing,
that He Who began a good work in *me*,
will continue until the day of Jesus Christ...
developing that good work and perfecting
and bringing it to full completion in *me*."
Philippians 1:6 *Amplified (personalized)*

I Am Always...

*N*ever again would our family be normal. I must accept this truth that the family as I had known it for over thirty years was gone. My Pollyanna nature could not promise that something wonderful was coming. Sadness darkened both days and nights; I was afraid of the future. Strong family relationships dissolved easily. Sobbing with a broken heart, I faintly, but surely, heard the Spirit's promises.

Barb, I am always...

Available	
Beside you	
Close	
Directing your path	Proverbs 3:6
Embracing you	
Freeing you	
Guarding your heart	
Holding your hand	
Inviting you to come closer	Matthew 11:28
J	
Keeping you safe	
Leading you	
Making you stronger	
Nearer than you can imagine	
Over your circumstances	
Present in this circumstance	
Quiet in My love	Zephaniah 3:17
Right here	
Setting your heart free	Psalm 119:32

Teaching you

Understanding   Psalm 103:14

Verifying who you are in Me

Waiting for you

X

Y

Z

The Lord never assured me things would be wonderful again; He only promised He would be with me through these moments.

"When I am afraid, I will trust in You."
Psalm 56:3

I Struggle to Believe in You

*B*irds and butterflies have always whispered to me of God's unfailing love; sunrises and sunsets paint messages of His delights. In those times I am alive with the truth that He chose me, "actually picked me out for Himself" (Ephesians 1:4 *Amplified*). It is easy to hear the whispers in the good days, when life is going as it should. What about the seasons without a sunrise or a bird song? When life hurts too much, Father, quiet my heart and hold my hand.

I struggle to believe in Your...

Affection for me

Banner over me

Constancy in this universe

Desire for me

Eternal-ness

Friendship

Gentleness

Holiness

Intimacy with me

Jealousy for all of me

King-liness

Love *(You love me!)*

Majestic power in a storm

Nearness

Oneness, in three

Purpose for me, for humanity

Quietness over me

Revelation to us

Sweetness

Timeliness in my circumstances

Understanding, when I don't know what is ahead

Victory

Ways

X

Yearning for me

Z

When times are good, be happy;
but when times are bad, consider:
God has made the one as well as the other.
Therefore, a man cannot discover
anything about his future."
Ecclesiastes 7:14

You Are Still the...

I can't do this again. I cannot go through any more heartbreak. Could our family survive another divorce? I wondered if God even cared. Tears blinded the road in front of me, but I could hear the whispered words, "Yes, you can." An argument followed between me and the Lord. I was just as determined I could not endure this. Gently, His truth calmed me, and I focused on His goodness. I know, I know, my Father.

Yes, I can because You are still the...

Abba of my life

Beginning and the End   Revelation 1:8

Creator

Designer

Exalted One

Faithful One

Giver of Grace and hope

Helper

Instrument of salvation

Justifier

Keeper of my soul

Lifter up of my life

Mighty One

Near One

Omnipresent One

Present Peace in my life

Quest of my soul

Restorer

Source of my Strength
    Safe place
Truth of my life
Unfailing One
Victorious One
Wise One
X-pected One
Yesterdays of life and the tomorrows
Zenith of life

God was, is, and will always be...

"I will never under any circumstances desert you
nor give you up nor leave you without support,
nor will I in any degree leave you helpless,
nor will I forsake or let you down
or relax My hold on you.
Assuredly not!"
Hebrews 13:5b *Amplified*

Come Just as You Are…

*T*ears painted ink spots on the journal page. I had been reading Psalm 15, and asked the same question David asked. "Lord, who may dwell in Your sanctuary? Who may live on Your holy hill?" I had begun the list as the Psalmist did; the blameless can, the honest are allowed in, the righteous may dwell in God's intimate presence. A quiet thought interrupted my religious ABC list. Surely there is another question to consider. Who can come to You, Father, just as they are? What do You say to those who feel they are not good enough? To those who want no part of You? What do You say to them? He whispers, "I know each one by name. I long for them to receive My love no matter the situation, the doubt, the choices. I want them to hear…"

I wait for you. Come to Me just as you are…

Abused

    Abandoned

Battered

    Broken   Burdened

Conflicted

    Condemned

Depressed

    Devastated   Doubting

Enveloped in pain

Fearful

Guilty

Heartbroken

    Hurting

Isolated

J

K

Lonely

Mad

Negative

Ostracized

Poor

Questioning

Rebellious

Scared

    Scarred   Searching   Sad

Traumatized

Useless

    Unloved   Unbelieving

Violent

Weary

    Worn

X

Y

Z

I cannot describe the pain surrounding me as this list came together. You see, I love someone very deeply who is wearing many of these ABC labels this moment.

> "Come to Me, all you who are weary and burdened,
> and I will give you rest. Take my yoke upon you
> and learn from Me, for I am gentle and humble in heart,
> and you will find rest for your souls.
> For my yoke is easy and my burden is light."
> Matthew 11:28-30

> "For God so loved the world…" John 3:16

WHISPERS IN YOUR HEARTBREAK

This is a page for you if you are going through a difficult, uncertain crisis. Your faith is shaken, and you are aware you must have a word, a positive word of His love and presence in your life during this time. The dark places on your journey weave doubt and confusion.

Use the ABCs as a guide to focus on the whispers you hear from your Father's heart. There is no expectation to complete the list — only an encouragement to hear gentle promises.

You may say, I am in despair, my Father. Enable me to believe You will... from A-Z; or you could say, I want to trust You completely, Father. I commit to... from A-Z.

_____ ◄ ◄

A _____

B _____

C _____

D _____

E _____

F _____

G _____

H _____

I _____

J _____

K _____

L _____

M _____

N _____

O _____

P _____

Q _____

R _____

S _____

T _____

U _____

V _____

W _____

X _____

Y _____

Z _____

"Most blessed is the man *(or woman)*
who believes in, trusts in, and relies on the Lord,
and whose hope and confidence the Lord is."
Jeremiah 17:7 *Amplified (personalized)*

... to live without listening at all is to live deaf
to the fullness of the music... He says He is with us
on our journeys. He says He has been with us
since each of our journeys began. Listen for Him.

The Sacred Journey, Frederick Buechner

Whispers to Personal Desires

Making a list of ABC words in praise or intercession may not be considered a "spiritual" experience for some. I had to find my way. As a young mother of four children, I spent much grief in "trying to have a quiet time". I would return from a conference with GUILTY stamped on my heart. The attendees were challenged to wake in the middle of the night to spend an hour alone or to set the clock an hour earlier before the hectic day began. Glorious benefits were touted, but I found only exhaustion and frustration.

Slowly, slowly... I learned to enjoy the moments, to pause for a spiritual whisper when there was a physical break. I shared the moments with my children — sunsets, sunrises, moon lit nights became sanctuaries for each one. This section of ABC lists does not fit into praise, thankfulness or heartbreak. These six lists are examples of surprise moments as I explored ways to hear and understand the Lord's direction in new areas of life.

You've been at a place with questions of why or how. Perhaps, now, you are cushioned between a mountain top of happiness and a plateau of sameness. You long to hear a whisper.

The following pages may trigger a thought or an idea as you listen to ABC words. Simply whisper your question or desire.

This is what the Lord says: "Stand at the crossroads and look;
ask for the ancient paths, ask where the good way is, and walk in it,
and you will find rest for your souls..."
Jeremiah 6:16a

*A*s a young pastor's wife, I needed to understand the truth of living in daily relationship with my heavenly Father. *Disciplines of a Beautiful Woman* by Anne Ortland, and *Lord, Change Me* by Evelyn Christenson coached me on my journey. Many other Christian authors reinforced the same principles necessary for a godly walk. I tucked them in my heart. Often when ironing, I would pray and use the ABCs.

*Oh, my Father,
I want to become a woman of...*

Awareness

Beauty

Confidence

    Courage

Discipline

Excellence

    Empathy

Faith

    Focus   Forgiveness

Generosity

Honesty

Integrity

Joy

Kindness

Laughter

Mystery

Nobility

Order

Passion

Patience

Quest

Respect

Strength

Transparency

Trust

Usefulness

Vision

Wisdom

X-pectancy

Yearning for You

Zeal

Similar lists of my longing to be a woman after God's heart appear often in my prayer journals.

"She speaks with wisdom,
and faithful instruction is on her tongue."
Proverbs 31:26

CREATE IN ME

*S*ymptoms triggered by Lyme disease altered my focus for an entire year. Sleepless nights, high blood pressure, and heart issues all caused fear and anxiety, changing my demeanor and outlook for life. As I responded to the prescribed treatment, my worn, worry-filled heart needed a transplant. The cry of David when he, too, acknowledged his need for a new heart, became my cry (Psalm 51:10).

Please, Lord,
Create in me a/an _____ heart...

Awe-filled

Believing

Balanced

Committed

Consecrated

Disciplined

Devoted

Eager

Faithful

Fearless

Gentle

Grateful

Hungry

Inviting

Joyful

Kind

Listening

Merry

Noble

Observant

   Obedient

Pure

   Peaceful   Praying

Quiet

Reverent

   Resting

Sacrificial

   Seeking

Thirsty

Understanding

Victorious

   Vast BIG heart to love

Welcoming

X-pectant

Yearning

Zealous

This list complete with twenty-six positive words makes me smile. Even as the previous months had centered on the negative, causing me despair, the Lord knew the desires of my heart.

> "I will give *her* an undivided heart
> and put a new spirit in *her*.
> I will remove from *her*... *her* heart of stone
> and give *her* a heart of flesh."
> Ezekiel 11:19 *(personalized)*

SEARCH ME

*W*ords exploded around me like bullets. Why would this list come together so quickly? Could it be that I am so human? I wanted to run and hide from such evil. I had read and made notes on Psalm 139 before walking that day. Innocently, or perhaps, pridefully, I began my trek asking the Lord to search me and know my heart... *(just perhaps maybe there could be one, or maybe two!)* to see if there is any offensive, wicked way in me *(verses 23 and 24)*.

Father, show me if I am...

Angry

    Arrogant

Boastful

Complaining

Deceitful

    Doubting

Exalted in self

Faultfinding

    Fake

Guilty of gossip

Haughty

Insistent for my way

    an Instigator

Judgmental

K

Lazy

Mocking

Nagging

Opinionated

Prejudiced

    Prideful

too Questioning

Rebellious

a Slanderer

    a Stumbling block

Two-faced

Uncompromising

Vain

    Vindictive

Worried

    Whiney   Wasteful

X

Y

Z

I am thankful no words for K, X, Y, and Z surfaced.

"If You, O Lord, kept a record of sins,
O Lord, who could stand?
But with You there is forgiveness;
therefore You are feared."
Psalm 130:3-4

I am scheduled to lead a seminar on marriage this morning. The afternoon is to be filled with conversations as the ladies share intimate situations with me. I had prayed my words for the presentation be honoring to the Lord. Now I asked that my personal conversations be pure and holy, as well. Early this cold February morning, I walked with this plea in my heart (Psalm 19:14).

Let the words of my mouth be...

Acceptable to You, O Lord

a Blessing to them

Caring

Defining

Encouraging

Friendly

Gracious

Helpful

full of Integrity

Joyful

Kind

Lacking in prejudice

Marked with wisdom

Never negative

In Obedience to You

Pleasant

    Pure

Quietly spoken

Restoring

Soft and gentle

Truthful

Unselfish

Very affirming

Without complaint

X-pressed in love

Yes in all ways possible

with Zeal

"Set a guard over my mouth, O Lord;
keep watch over the door of my lips."
Psalm 141:3

How I Show the Lord I Love Him

*F*or days I had asked HOW... how can I show You, Lord, that I love You? Jesus quoted verse five of Deuteronomy chapter six when He was asked by an expert in the law what the greatest commandment was... "Love the Lord your God with all your heart and with all your soul and with all your strength." The words for HOW came quickly through tears as I realized how often I fail in showing my love.

How can I show the Lord that I love Him? I can...

Acknowledge who He is in my life

Believe His words

Commit this day to Him

Dwell with Him *(that is, to make myself at home with Him!)*

Exalt Him

Forgive others *(this shows I love the Lord)*

Give generously

Hide His word in my heart

Intentionally live to please Him

Joy in His presence

Kneel in adoration, in heart, soul and mind

Learn His ways

Magnify His name

Never forget His sacrifice for me

Obey His commandments

Pursue a more intimate relationship with Him

Quiet my mind at His feet

Receive His gifts gratefully

Serve in His name

Teach my children and grandchildren His ways

Unite with other believers

Vow to keep His Word in my heart

Walk daily with Him

X

Yearn for Him constantly

Z

"And this is love;
that we walk in obedience to His commands.
As you have heard from the beginning,
His command is that you walk in love."
2 John 1:6

I See Him Everywhere

*P*ages in my journal are filled with practical ways I show the Lord I love Him or ways I understand His love for me. Psalm 42:8 is noted at the top of this list: "By day the Lord directs His love, at night His song is with me — a prayer to the God of my life." I sense God in daily, ordinary life events. His presence is near, in the moments.

I see Him everywhere...

in an Abundance of mercy

in a Butterfly's delicate wings

in a Cross painted in the sky by contrails from an airplane

as Dawn erupts, and He says, "I am here in this day."

in the Embraces of the wind

in the Fragrance of flowers *(I smell every rose I meet!)*

in the Grace of another's forgiveness of me

in the Helping Hands of others

with Instruction in the night   Psalm 16:7

in those Joy people I have in life

in the Kindness of a stranger

in the Laughter of my grandchildren

in the Magic of Music

in the Nights, He sings over me in the darkness   Psalm 42:8

O

with Peace in the difficult moments

in the Quiet moments of His nearness   Psalm 46:10

in the Raindrops on the dry earth

in Sunrises and Sunsets

in Tom's love... pure, sweet, complete

in Uncertainty, He says, "Trust Me"

in the Vastness of the ocean, sensing His infiniteness

in His Whispers through pain

X

Y

in a Zero, never-ending, complete in Him

How do you sense God's presence? Your list would be different, as special and beautiful as you are.

"If I go up to the heavens, You are there;
if I make my bed in the depths, You are there.
If I rise on the wings of the dawn,
if I settle on the far side of the sea,
even there Your hand will guide me,
Your right hand will hold me fast."
Psalm 139:8-10

... Christianity is more than a theory about the universe,
more than teachings written down on paper;
it is a path along which we journey —
in the deepest and richest sense,
the way of life.

The Orthodox Way, Kallistos Ware

SECTION FIVE

Whispers in the Study of God's Word

This method of applying the ABCs in Bible study presents an interesting glimpse into various characters' lives. I read a passage several times, inspecting every detail... listening, observing, thinking, sensing the dynamics in the story. Immersed in the story and the culture for days, I feel I know them personally.

I was a 'fly on the wall' in the living room with Mary and in the kitchen with Martha (Luke 10). I imagined Jesus' encounter with the woman at the well (John 4). Focusing on words for the alphabet is not at all like an in depth study of a Hebrew or Greek word or passage. For me, it is an experience in understanding people and the times; it's a way to observe actions and conversation to discover just how they might have been. Discovering words for a trait, an emotion or a particular characteristic, I come to see the one I studied as a real person... just as I am.

This type of New Testament study, concentrating on one character at a time using the ABCs, has helped me see Jesus' heart for the world. Clearly His desire is to change each one of us.

There are two lists in this section from Luke 10, one of Mary and one of Martha. I think you will identify with the heart of both sisters. You may notice other characteristics as you focus on the Scripture.

You will find a page to study the woman at the well (John 4) using the ABC focus.

MARY OF BETHANY

I ponder Mary, the sister of Martha and Lazarus, sitting at the feet of Jesus (Luke 10:38-42). What was she thinking? Did she have expectations of what He might say? Did she even hear Martha stirring up louder than normal noises in the kitchen? What stirred within her heart as she focused on the words of her Master? I am here this morning at His feet, hungering for His presence, His touch.

Like Mary, I wait with...

Anticipation

Belief

Calmness

>Contentment

Devotion

>Delight

Excitement

Focus

Gratitude

Hunger

Imagination

Joy

K

Love

Music ringing in my heart

N

Obedience

Peace

Quietness

Readiness

Serenity

Tears

an Undivided heart

V

Wonder

X-pectancy

Yearning

Z

I want to hear the whispers of Martha's heart, too. That list will be next. Then I want you to try one on your own with the woman at the well (John 4).

"Mary has chosen what is better,
and it will not be taken away from her."
Luke 10:42

*M*artha is the other sister in this story. I believe she loved Jesus as much as Mary did. Have you ever wondered how many times she opened her home to Him and to His disciples? Martha is often compared to Mary, her 'more spiritual' sister. As you spend time with Martha, you sense her longing... and her busyness. You identify with her. A study with the ABCs uncovers many positive traits, as well as negative ones. We realize she is as human as you and I are. But with all her goodness, she needed more time at His feet. Did she desire to serve Jesus more than she wanted to commune with Him? I find Martha a kindred spirit!

Martha was...

Adaptable

    Amiable

Busy

Conscientious

Demanding

Envious

Friendly

Generous

Hospitable

    Hyper

Industrious

    Insecure

Just

K

Loving

Meticulous

N

Organized

Prepared

    Pre-occupied

Quite the cook!

    (Can you imagine serving the Messiah lunch?)

Rigid

Strong

Tired

Useful

    Upset

V

Worried

X

Y

Z

Tonight I was chopping celery in the kitchen (with Martha). Hearing whispers in the living room, I thought for a moment of running in there to sit in quietness. I kept chopping...

Forgive me, Lord, when I am more noisy in the kitchen than quiet in Your presence.

"Martha, Martha," the Lord answered,
"you are worried and upset about many things,
but only one thing is needed."
Luke 10:41

THE WOMAN AT THE WELL

I encourage you to spend time with the Samaritan woman in the fourth chapter of John. She walks fast as she doesn't want to meet anyone on her way to fill her water jars. Why? Imagine the afternoon is hot, the road is dusty. What is she afraid of? Feel her pain... her guilt? This is a great study of this woman's encounter with Jesus. Using the ABCs as a guide, begin a 'before and after' list to discover a beautiful picture of a changed life.

Draw on your imagination from the story and your knowledge of New Testament culture. Sense the heartache of this woman. Remember, you will focus on words or phrases using the ABCs. Listen for whispers from this passage to better understand Jesus' heart for the world.

Her journey before...   After she met Jesus...

A _____	A _____
B _____	B _____
C _____	C _____
D _____	D _____
E _____	E _____
F _____	F _____
G _____	G _____
H _____	H _____
I _____	I _____
J _____	J _____
K _____	K _____
L _____	L _____
M _____	M _____
N _____	N _____

O _____	O _____
P _____	P _____
Q _____	Q _____
R _____	R _____
S _____	S _____
T _____	T _____
U _____	U _____
V _____	V _____
W _____	W _____
X _____	X _____
Y _____	Y _____
Z _____	Z _____

I would love for you to complete the above two lists as much as you can — the before and after. Then you can peek at my completed list on the next page.

"Come, see a man who told me everything
I ever did. Could this be the Christ?"
John 4:29

THE WOMAN AT THE WELL

I wish John had written more details in this story. But then there would be no need for me to use my imagination into her life and into Jesus' heart. See the life and heart of this woman with whom Jesus had a special appointment. Can you imagine her pain and guilt as she runs to fill her water jars before she meets anyone on her daily trip?

Her journey before...   After she met Jesus...

Angry, Adulteress, Ashamed	Amazed, Accepted, Alive
Begging, Blaming, Bold	Blessed, Believed
Critical	Compassionate, Changed
Doubting, in Despair	Dancing *(I think she danced!)*
Easily Enticed	E
Friendless	Forgiven, Free
Guilty	Given Grace
Hopeless, Honest	Hopeful
Intimidated	Included, Inviting others
Joyless	Joyful
Knowledgeable	Kind
Lonely	Loved
Miserable	Moved to action
Needy	N
Ostracized	Observant
Paranoid	Passionate
Questioning	Quick to respond
Respectful	Restored
Sad, Scared, Surprised	Sharing

Thirsty, Tainted	Thankful
Unfulfilled	Unashamed
Void, vexed	Victorious
Weary	a Witness
X	X
Y	Y
Z	Z

Why did the townspeople believe her so quickly? She represents a changed life!

"Come, see a man who told me everything
I ever did. Could this be the Christ?"
John 4:29

About the Author

Barb Suiter has always enjoyed moments in nature. Living in Tennessee's countryside with Tom, her retired pastor husband, provides daily amazement of butterflies and birds. Graduating with honors at forty-one from Valdosta State University, Georgia, with an English/Journalism degree, Barb is a life-long journaler and now a blogger. She taught English as a Second Language for years, including classes at Vanderbilt University, as well as English classes during their years as missionaries.

While Tom ministered in Mississippi, Georgia, Tennessee, and Europe for fifty years, Barb was always active in Women's Ministry, teaching women's studies and creating a home filled with love and children. Their ministry journey included a decade (2000-2010) with the International Mission Board, in Vienna, Austria and Copenhagen, Denmark. Those years serving international churches and leading Biblical studies at the United Nations in Vienna were the watershed of their long ministry.

Barb and Tom have four children, thirteen grandchildren (one of whom illustrated this book), and four great-grandchildren! An eager gardener, Barb's blog often shares spiritual truths learned while gardening and listening to quiet whispers. This creates a daily dilemma — she doesn't know whether to weed or write!

You can keep up with Barb's most recent projects on her blog at
https://ajourneytonow.me

About the Illustrator

Sarah Dean, one of Barb's grandchildren, began art classes for fun when she was eleven years old. To her surprise, she enjoyed her assignments in various areas of creative art and won several awards in photography. Sarah is currently a freshman at Ouachita Baptist University in Arkadelphia, Arkansas.

A Source for My Healing

About Barb's next book...

It was not easy to believe, simply believe, I was loved and accepted by an awesome big God. I came to understand this was so hard because my father had destroyed the concept of a father's good love. As a victim of childhood sexual abuse at the hands of my preacher father, I could not translate God's love to me. There must be something terribly evil in me.

Yes, I trusted my husband Tom loved me, but he wasn't my father. Slowly I learned to grasp maybe, just maybe, this God could love me if Tom could.

I journeyed through the years allowing words of affirmation and love from these ABC lists to lodge in empty, hurtful places in my mind, conscious and subconscious. I learned to trust God's whispers.

Now in my senior years, I am convinced my journey hearing the very whispers of God have brought complete healing from my father's abuse. The ABC method has been a source for my healing.

I am often asked 'how?' I have lived a life of purpose, of a contentment resulting in a healthy, happy marriage. This practice of walking with the Lord in praise, intercession and confession is one of the gifts I have opened. I share more of this journey of moving from scared and scarred to sacred in a book currently being written. The book will explore the process of healing from wounds of childhood sexual trauma. For more information about this book, please follow my blog at https://ajourneytonow.me.

ALSO FROM SEVEN INTERACTIVE

*Called To Reign: The Bride of Christ
and the Unfolding Story of God's Kingdom People*
by Rick Edwards

Called To Reign is a study of who we are as the people of God, what He has in store for us, and how we are to live as the Bride of Christ, but it's also a call for the local church to teach the story of God's kingdom deliberately and strategically. For many, the Bible is little more than an ancient collection of random stories that are disconnected and largely irrelevant. Church educators and Christian publishers often foster this misconception (inadvertently) by developing curriculum plans that study isolated biblical texts but never consider the broader narrative of the Bible. Rick Edwards, a pastor, publisher, and Christian educator, argues that the ancient Hebrew wedding, as understood by Jesus and the biblical writers, provides a model for understanding the biblical story and, consequently, all of human history. *Called To Reign* can be found on Amazon.com.

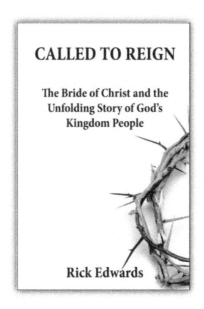